TRANSFORM YOUR BAD HABITS TO BETTER BEHAVIOR PATTERNS

Learn Helpful Tips To Stop Destructive Habits Such As How To Stop Drinking Alcohol On Your Own And How To Get Rid Of Nervous Habits Such As Fingernail Biting So You Can Make Better Changes To Improve The Quality Of Your Life

By:

Bessie K. Redman
Copyright 2010

Habits are regular patterns of behavior. You do them automatically, often without thinking about it. Habits, whether good or bad become innate to us, therefore they somehow form who we are.

Bad habits can be very hard to break. If we are determined though, we can control them and make better changes to improve our life. There are steps to take in order to break a bad habit. This book will give some very helpful tips, here is a preview:

1. Form the right mindset. Just like learning a new skill requires commitment and determination, so does getting rid of a bad habit. When you are fixed with a purpose to change for the better, then you will be able to bring it about.

2. Identify your trigger factors. Study yourself and your behavior. Take some time to watch your behavior attentively. Take note of what triggered your actions and reactions under certain conditions. Write down your observations so you can organize your behavioral patterns.

3. After you've identified and organized your behavior, you will see certain patterns come up. This is self-awareness. Now, that you are aware of certain trigger factors and situations, you can now devise a plan of action to form alternative behaviors which you can practice on to rid yourself of your bad habits.

Contents

Bad Study Habits 3
Kids And Bad Habits 6
Bad Habits In Relationships 9
Bad Habits In Sports-Killing The True Spirit 12
Bad Habits Related To Health 15
Dangerous Bad Habits 17
Financial Bad Habits 20
Illegal Bad Habits 23
Irritating Bad Habits 26
Social Bad Habits 29
Avoiding Bad Habits 32
Nicotine Withdrawal: Simple Solution For Smokers 35
How Good Habits Can Turn Into Bad Habits 37
Bad Habits Can Be Expensive 39
Medical Treatments For Bad Habits 42
Research About Bad Habits 45

Bad Study Habits

If you are in high school or college, you know that you will not get the best grades if you have bad study habits. Unless you are a naturally gifted student, it takes some effort to get the grade point average you need to continue in your academic career. Even if you are gifted, bad habits can hurt your scores.

Of course, the worst of the bad habits of studying is not studying at all. Some people plan to go through school without cracking open a book. It is rare for this to be an adequate response to academia. Most people need to study.

Some people do not go to class. This is another bad habit. The teacher or professor may give you information that if not in any of the literature. To get it, it is best to go to class. You might be able to get it second hand from someone who did go to class, but there is nothing like hearing it for yourself.

Sometimes students go to class, but they go unprepared. Some do not buy the proper literature or lab materials. They try to get by with sharing or looking on others' work. This is a bad habit, as they will not get the personal experience that they would with their own literature and materials.

You can buy the right literature and lab materials, but if you do not have the right equipment and supplies. You will suffer if you do not have the right supplies to go along with it. If you make it a habit to show up without paper, pen, pencil, or even a laptop computer if needed, you will not be able to do your work.

There are certain physical bad habits that make studying harder. Studying without eating is like trying to drive a car without fuel-it does not work very well. Studying without sleep is unproductive. Studying with a hangover is very distracting.

Many students will go to class to be entertained. This seems almost reasonable because many professors have great senses of humor. However serious learning should be taking place as well. If you find yourself not taking notes, you will know you are slipping into bad habits. If you get to class and you have not read the assignment, you will be ill prepared.

Cramming for tests is a time honored tradition. Yet, if you want to retain the material beyond the end of the semester, it is a bad habit to start. Doing daily work will help you to understand the material that is being put into your brain. It will help you assimilate it in a way that will help you to remember it in the long haul.

If you are a motivated student, your bad habits may be just as unproductive, in the short run at least. You may find yourself straying in your research. You find your subjects fascinating, but you find other information interesting as well. Before you know it, you have spent hours on the internet researching something you do not need for your school work at all. It may increase your knowledge overall, but it will not help today.

You can rid yourself of your bad habits when you are studying or preparing to study. Some people choose not to. However, you might find it beneficial.

Kids And Bad Habits

Kids go through periods of having bad habits. Some of their bad habits are worrisome and some are just really annoying. Parents agonize over what to do about their children's unacceptable behaviors. There are a few things they should know.

1. What you see as bad habits may actually be natural stages of child development. If your very young child is examining the lint between his toes regularly, you might think it is a bad habit. It might be, though, that the child simply finds toe lint interesting. The child will outgrow the fascination and the bad habit will disappear.

2. So-called bad habits may be ways for the child to soothe themselves. At times when they would ordinarily feel like screaming and crying, they may suck on their clothes instead. This makes them feel calm and secure.

3. Children may use bad habits to feel a sense of control over their environment. If they are dropped off at a daycare center for the first time, they may start having odd behaviors. This could be, for instance, rubbing the material of their clothing. As time goes by, if the daycare center continues to feel threatening to them, rubbing the clothing material could become a bad habit.

4. Kids sometimes do things adults see as bad habits that they do not understand. Sometimes, the kids are simply solving a problem. If their hands are cold, they may put them between their legs to warm them up. Adults often misinterpret this and overreact. If they knew the problem was cold hands, they might have a different solution to offer.

5. Shaming and punishment are the worst things you can do. If a child is doing the bad habits in an effort to soothe herself, making her feel bad is counterproductive. It will give her more to self-soothe about. This is why parents often become frustrated when trying to deal with a child's bad habits.

6. Substituting more pleasant behaviors for the annoying or destructive bad habits can work better. You can teach your child to be aware of when they are doing a bad habit. Then, you can teach them another behavior to do instead. When they do, reward them.

7. Incentives work to help some older children get over bad habits. This is especially true if they are old enough to think in the long term of at least a few weeks. You can offer them a reward every day that they do not do their bad habits. By the time they have quit, they will have a large reward waiting.

8. Usually, the best thing you can do is to wait for the bad habits to go away all on their own. As long as you do not reinforce the bad habits by doing them yourself, the kids should grow out of them. Once they get older, their school

mates will make it more attractive to them to stop doing their bad habits. Kids like to fit in.

The most important thing to remember about your child's bad habits is that you should not be too alarmed. Only when they are destructive or dangerous is it essential for you to stop them immediately. Otherwise, be understanding and gentle when dealing with your kid's bad habits.

Bad Habits In Relationships

There exist bad habits in every quarter of life, bad habits in relationships are annoying and lead to distorted relationships. Even if a person is truly interested in making a relationship work, such bad habits curb the progress. The bad habits in relationships are many.

Jealousy is one thing that murders every other relationship. A girlfriend might be suspected by her boyfriend, that she goes around with men, whom she really doesn't need to. And other one is when a woman keeps imagining that her husband is looking for some other woman to fill her place. This is just a bad habit that can be overcome. It is something virtual.

Another bad habit is not listening to a person when he/she is talking. People need to respond when one is trying to explain something to them, this is called selective hearing. Though people respond with a YES for the things told by us, they are not really listening.

Another thing is when a person tries to converse with another person about something they both like, the second person takes complete control of the conversation and this might actually prove disastrous even for a friendly relationship.

The long running relationships manage to culminate a couple of bad habits among people. When one person is too dependent on their partner, they end up losing the ability to look after themselves. This can actually affect them at work. This cripples their efficiency, because they know someone to actually back them. This is a really bad habit that will have its effects later.

Yelling at your partner for differences in opinion is also a bad habit that crops up in healthy relationships. All couples argue over an issue at some point of time. But creating a fuss over the issue will kill the relationship.

Bringing up old issues while arguing with your partner is something that is not suggested, this will leave a bad taste in both their mouths. The differences in opinion must be resolved by sensible arguments and must not be carried on from time to time with constant disagreements.

Nagging is something that can irritate anyone, whether it be for a girl or a guy, it sure turns people off if their partner is going to constantly nag him/her for doing something. This is something that is majorly seen as a girl thing. This leads to bad relationships.

Blaming your partner is like blaming yourself. So, you will have an effect on anything that they do. Generally, it is one person who blames all the time, and the other person takes it all. This takes the relationship to a path downhill.

When people blame at their partners constantly, it leads to a situation where the distance between the two gets increased more than what they imagine. They will lose trust on other people also.

The quicker people manage to get out of such bad habits, the better it is, for their relationship. Everyone expects their partners to be understanding and caring. If any of these bad habits rule a person's mind, it is going to be hard to keep the relationship going.

Bad Habits In Sports-Killing The True Spirit

The bad habits involved in sportsmen need to be curbed in order to enjoy the game. The pathway to victory is laid by the behavior patterns that need to be developed in every sportsman. Avoiding bad habits plays a major part in this.

Booze and cigarettes are two things that kill not only the sport, but also the sportsman. These two are the main things that need to be curbed in order to play any game effectively. The breathing capability of a sportsman gets decreased badly if he keeps smoking all the time, this will lead to a situation where they have to gasp for fresh air even after a sprint.

Influence of alcohol is something that is not supposed to be there for athletes. It leads to a situation where the body is dehydrated. It is necessary to consume other fluids. Keeping oneself hydrated is something important. The drinks that provide plenty of electrolytes keep the sportsmen in form.

Sleep and proper rest are most important for sportsmen. After they wind up at practice, they need to get back home for enough rest to relax the muscles that were flexed. Practicing after a good sleep will always enhance their performance. Lack of sleep in turn has extreme effects that will curb their efficiency.

Warm-up and stretching are most important for athletes. They should never run before they are sure that their warm up was enough. The warm-up sessions always help the relaxed muscles to get ready for the flexing. This is one thing that amateur people are really careless about.

People who do not take any sport seriously and dream of becoming athletes in a day will get injured and will end up exhausting themselves. It is always necessary to practice to be good in any sport. It is highly impossible to run in a race and win without any practice.

Not using the right safety equipments that need to be used is a bad habit. The absence of the right protection gear in professional sports will be noted and a fine would be levied on the player who is not following those rules.

Amateurs who play games like golf don really bother about the shoe that they are wearing. It is necessary to wear a golf shoe in order to prevent yourself from slipping and falling. And in bicycling, the usage of helmet is mandatory, but amateur riders don't follow it.

Not being a team player is something that is really bad and needs to be attended immediately. In games that need to be played as a team, people make the mistake of being selfish in order to take the thunder off others. Any team will be victorious if all the players in the team think positively and play as a team.

Bad habits that can be curbed in order to keep the spirit of the game alive need to be attended to and kicked out of the system immediately. This will make everyone including the person playing sit up and enjoy the game. This is how the whole concept works.

Bad Habits Related To Health

There are many bad habits that damage a person's health. They can give you the feeling that you are not healthy. They affect the physical condition of a person. In order to lead a long and healthy life, there are certain things that need to be strictly followed.

Bad habits related to eating make you feel uncomfortable. Surveys have shown that many people in the United States of America are obese. Overeating is the phenomenon behind this.

Problems related to heart, diabetes, bone disorder and joint disorder, are all a result of overeating or improper diet. This can also lead to other physical problems. This can even result in some kind of cancer with the obese people. Nowadays, obese people are bedridden and they cannot take care of themselves.

Leave alone overeating, even not sticking to a proper diet is something that is not good. Eating the wrong things at the wrong time, but sticking to a certain calorie diet, will also lead to this kind of situation. The habit of eating fast food during every meal is a bad habit. The quantities of sugars, fats and starches provided by the fast food, make people unhealthy.

Fried foods are bad for the health. It is fine to eat it at times, but not good all the time. Foods that don't have enough fiber in them are also a bad habit that prevents the body from not functioning well. Foods that have high sugar content are addictions. The metabolism of the body gets affected drastically. This leads to a situation where there is an insulin imbalance.

The right electrolytes, when not given to the body also cause some trouble. Adding too much salt to any food is also a bad habit. Salting all the foods will lead to a situation called hypertension.

Eating is not the only thing; the lack of exercise is also a bad habit. If your job does not allow you to move around regularly, then all the food you consumed is going to take longer time to digest. It is always good to walk around after a good meal.

It is always good to exercise regularly. It is a bad habit not to do so. Apart from this, working too much is also not good for the health. It leads to heart disease, blood pressure, and many other problems if we don't relax for a while.

Booze, Cigarettes, Joints, these are really bad for the health. The health guide is not complete without them. These lead to a situation where people get addicted to it. The other risks involved in these are lung cancer, for smoking, liver damage, for drinking and brain hemorrhage for drugs.

Kicking out the bad habits in the system and leading a healthy life is something that everyone needs to aspire for. It is worth the try, because they will let you live longer than you thought you would. The existence of bad habits will only curb your efficiency and health, so, take care of your health!

Dangerous Bad Habits

There are bad habits that just annoy everyone, the rest are dangerous. Those kinds lead you to some sort of trouble. Some people take risks. The rest, do not care about the ways their bad habits influence others.

The worst form of bad habits comes in the form of not paying correct attention to the physical condition. It is really harmful to use sedating drugs. It is highly dangerous to work in two jobs with literally no sleep. It is always necessary to get good sleep before you get back to work.

The other form comes with electricity. People go to the extent of using damaged extension cords, not bothering about the outcome. Such usage can actually lead to fire or electrocution. Metal ladders near power lines are ladders to heaven; it is a very dangerous habit.

Some people have habits that are far beyond your capability of thinking how bad it is. Many people from the younger generation find it cool to stand on cars, when they are moving. This is more sort of an irresponsible behavior than coolness. It can lead to death.

There are many bad habits that are followed when driving a car. It can be fatal when they are not sensible when they are driving. Now, the bad habit has been put to use very frequently that they don't even realize that it is a bad habit. This leads to unpleasant situations.

Some women have the bad habit of grooming themselves. This, when done while driving, is really dangerous. They are dumb enough to believe that they can watch the road while applying mascara. This might work out at times, but a time will come when they will crash their car in the truck that is coming from the opposite direction.

Not leaving the men, some men try to shave while riding, this is as weird as applying mascara while driving. Another thing is combing their hair, which can again lead to an accident. Another frequently repeated mistake is using the mobile phones while driving. When people start using their mobile phone while riding, they concentrate more on the phone than the person in front, which paves the way to hell.

Driving through water is a bad habit. This does not make one braver, but makes the situation graver. Apart from that, driving through water damages your car badly, it takes several months for your car to get back to the normal position.

Drinking and driving not only makes you spill your beer, but also makes you spill your brain. This is a suicidal act that can put another person's life at stake. What if an infant or an elderly person just get knocked down? This bad habit can make you feel guilty for a long. Drunken driving can actually end you up in jail.

Any habit that actually puts others and your life at stake is a bad habit! The more you get addicted to the bad habit, more is the chance of you killing yourself and another person. So, learn about your bad habits and try to curb them!

Financial Bad Habits

Getting into financial bad habits is not at all a big deal; it is one of the easiest to get to. Some people are so full of money that they can buy anything without any sort of apprehension. But, it is always suggested that people stay vigilant and keep the expenses down.

Credit cards encourage financial bad habits. Some people have the bad habit of buying too many things with their cards. It is very easy to get the credit card. There are so many companies offering credit cards, which do not ask you to hold much money in your bank account, which only adds fuel to fire.

These credit card companies do not seem to understand that their clients will have to pay other companies if they hold too many credit cards. Some of us get the cards keeping in mind the emergencies. But we end up spending a lot more than we know, using these credit cards. This leads to a situation where it will be hard for a person to pay even the minimal monthly payment.

This would lead to the next link in the chain, borrowing money from known people, especially acquaintances. That is just another bad habit. The relatives might want to help you, but not all the time. You cannot afford to look up to your relative to save your skin each and every time. This will again make you get back to square one.

The same thing applies even for friends. It is bad to lend or borrow money from them. This will only put a strain on the friendly relationship. One might even forget how much he borrowed. Borrowing money from friends is a bad habit that you can hardly quit.

Spending as per an economical budget is another thing that needs to be followed by everyone to keep away from being a spendthrift. This will give a basic idea as to where most of the money has been spent. It is always better to maintain the accounts on paper rather than trusting your brains with this. This will give precise information on the money being spent.

It is actually bad to be looking for the grace period, instead of paying up before the due date. Many people actually wait till the grace time turns up. Most of the utility companies give a grace period before they cut the service. Not paying up regularly might lead to a situation where the service might be cut off. This will also curb your credit rating.

Another bad habit is destroying the soft copy of the accounts before it can be copied into the system. This can be disastrous in a long run. It can be thrown away once you are sure that it has been noted. It is always good to hold a record of all the withdrawals and deposits. And it is safe to keep accurate information in the form of debit slips and ATM.

It is a bad habit not to reconcile the accounts. It is really safe and an easy way out if people follow the internet banking facility provided by all banks. It is always safe to keep an eye on your account to prevent any kind of fraud. These financial habits will be a saving grace amongst the other bad habits followed by us.

Illegal Bad Habits

Not all bad habits are legal, some make even the system turn back to look at you, and they are termed illegal. Those cannot be merely pushed off saying that they are bad habits. They are illegal, and bad, and happen quite frequently, so they are more or less some kind of habit.

Street fights, fisticuffs, and any fight that can actually hurt someone is a bad habit. These kinds of fights lead to arrests and even convictions. This is a result of people not thinking before they make a move to act. Destructive thoughts plague human mind, and when someone with all sorts of destructive feeling fights another person, it can be fatal.

Fights in bars are really common; this is quite a phenomenon there. Men, who are semi conscious with all the alcohol running down their bloodstream and the kick up their brain, don't even realize what they are doing. There are not many sensible people in that place to even stop the fight. The fights in their inebriated state can even lead to death.

The absence of enough places to sit, also leads to unwanted fights. Going to bars which are known for fisticuffs and verbal wars is a bad habit itself.

The cruelest bad habit that can be inculcated in any person is the domestic violence meted out to their partners. Some men do not hesitate to even physically abuse their wife who is pregnant. This act is more or less out of momentary anger.

Transactions that are not listed are illegal, and they are terrible bad habits. Gambling is an addiction, the more you win, the more you want. And at the end of it, you will lose it all. Regulated gambling is fine, and it takes place in a particular place in the state. And abiding by the laws and restrictions of the game will keep you away from the prison. Such a regulated gambling will prevent you from being swooped off all your money.

The younger generation kids are getting involved in malpractices like shoplifting, which is a terrible bad habit. Shoplifting is too hard to quit. It is an addiction again; you tend to slip things under your coat that actually will have bad influence on the generations to come. It is a disgrace in case you get caught red handed.

The habit of using others' money for personal purposes is a bad habit. It is easy to actually do it but then, it will grow upon you and land you in jail sometime in the near future.

Arsons are created by people obsessed with pleasure in killing and destroying others' life and property. Some arsonists fancy fire and they set buildings on fire and derive some sort of pleasure from that. Generally, an arson damages properties, and arsonists with such twisted mind create more damage.

Sometimes, our bad habits can be harsher on others' life. This might cause damage to others' property or even ruin their peace of mind. In order to secure a good name in the society, one has to curb these habits.

Irritating Bad Habits

Though people don't intend to, many of our bad habits irritate people. These habits often irk many people and they try to stop you themselves after you cross a limit. Though some of them are thoughtless behaviors, the rest are nervous habits.

Shopping brings out many bad habits in people. It is really bad to follow someone up to the parking lot and wait right behind them for the parking space. This will only make them feel like someone is forcing them, and this may make things worse if that person is going to find it hard to take the car out. This will irritate them more than they can take.

Another thoughtless behavior is when you cut through a line in a store where there are people waiting before you already. People will be thoroughly pissed off with such a selfish behavior and you might end up giving them a bad impression.

People tend to behave in a cranky manner when it comes to the queue they choose. People might get into an express line, where they are not supposed have more than 15 items, they might barge into that line with more than 15 items. Such behavior only gives others the wrong impression and they might get irritated after sometime.

Some of the most irritating nervous bad habits are listed. Cracking the knuckles by someone can be irritating for others. This can actually get on their nerves. The ones listening have to keep looking for the next crack sound from the knuckles.

Tapping a pencil, drumming on the desk, tapping the feet are all behaviors that can be enjoyed by you, but can be really annoying to others. Tapping a pencil during a test can really get on others' nerves; it will make it hard for them to concentrate. These are bad habits that come out of happiness and just a small leash can actually make you understand that it is bad.
Grinding the teeth is something that no one likes listening to. These are other bad habits that are related to noise. Clicking/ grinding the teeth. Smacking one's lips is not the best of sound that one would want to listen to.
Popping the chewing gum is a bad habit related to sound, and it is really annoying. To be more frank, it can drive people crazy. Leaving the faucet dripping is something that can actually irritate people who don't like it unclean. If someone has to go around looking for dripping faucets, it is going to be really annoying.

The dog barking is another thing that can get on people's nerves. The situation is worse if it happens during the night, when people around are sleeping. Sometimes, it is with some reason, but many a times, the reason is missing. There are solutions for this, which will keep the dogs quiet, and helps the neighbors sleep better, after a long day.

Breaking these irritating bad habits are really hard. The best part is that, some people, unaware of the situation tend to irritate others. But, if they actually try, it might help and they might stop following some of the bad habits. It will do a lot more good to the people around them, if they can actually stop following what is bad!

Social Bad Habits

Having bad habits in social situations can make you a very unpopular person. You may not even know how others feel about your social blunders. However, if you are acting in ways that are not considered appropriate, people will notice.

Many bad habits can be noticed when people go out to a restaurant together. It can be a very unpleasant experience if people have certain bad habits. For instance, chewing with an open mouth can be disgusting to the person watching. When a person does this, it is a thoughtless gesture.

Some people have the bad habits of eating other peoples' food. They will just reach over and take a bite of something on their neighbor's plate. They do not consider the fact that the person might want to be asked first. They do not take into account that the person might find it repulsive to share food with someone who has already used their fork.

Loudness in a restaurant is a bad habit that is sometimes appropriate and sometimes is not. In some settings, loudness is the order of the day. In quiet restaurants, though, a person needs to leave the volume turned to a low level. They need to try to fit in with the ambience of the restaurant.

Have you ever heard someone belch, and then say "not bad manners, just good food"? Well, it is bad manners, and bad habits, too. Nobody wants to hear that, and it is not excused by an attempt at humor. Some people seem to do this every time they feel the urge without thought to how others feel.

One of the sickening bad habits people have at restaurants is blowing their noses in a cloth napkin. It is not appropriate to blow their nose at the table in the first place. When they use a cloth napkin, the waiter cannot just throw it away. It has to be handled in order to be washed and reused. It is an inconsiderate bad habit.

Some parents have bad habits when it comes to their children's public behavior. Some will let their children run through the restaurant doing as they please. They will not say a word when their children misbehave. This can spoil an otherwise nice evening.

Other parents are so harsh and critical with their children that it also destroys any chance of anyone having a good time. These are bad habits just as letting the kids be destructive are. Ideally, parents can find a middle ground.

There are also bad habits that affect the way people feel about themselves. If you are a know-it-all, a person might feel inferior to you at first. Eventually, though, it will get old and they will resent you. If you are tactless, you can hurt peoples' feelings without thinking. You do it just because you are in the habit of "telling the truth."

There are bad habits that affect the way you communicate with others in the social setting. Monopolizing the conversation may make you feel good, but others will feel unappreciated. Interrupting can be a bad habit that prevents you from developing closeness with acquaintances.

Correct your bad habits in social situations and you will find that people are friendlier with you. You will see that good habits will get you much more good attention than bad habits.

Avoiding Bad Habits

Prevention is better than cure, is an apt saying for bad habits, it is always better to avoid them, rather than get started and later quit. Bad habits are inevitable, and there are too many to even think of staying away from. But still, keeping it low is the next best option.

One of the few main bad habits that should be strictly avoided is smoking. The nicotine and tar content from the cigarettes are something that leaves your body like a dump of waste. It is really easy to take the first puff off the cigarette, but it is the hardest to quit.

Other bad habits include bad eating schedule. The fear of gaining several pounds leaves people thinking whether to eat or not, though eating cannot be stopped completely, the lack of healthy food not only makes you thin, but also completely disease prone. So, it is your skill to limit your food in such a way that it keeps you healthy.

There are more positive ways to prevent you from becoming obese. Food, if seen as something special that you don't get very often, it will help. This basically lies in your choosing skills, if you choose to eat the best in the lot and leave the rest, it might help. The methods that can be followed to keep you away from becoming fat are many.

Exercise is a good habit, the lack of it, is surely a bad one. The need to walk around from one place is as good as a person looking for water when he is terribly thirsty, the absence of both at the right time, kills. Energy factor comes into play now, so, start off slowly, it increases your energy level gradually.

A good and a positive routine can always help you avoid bad habits concerned to personal hygiene. The basic personal hygiene practices are taking bath every morning, brushing your teeth when needed, and combing the hair while making an appearance in public. It reflects your personal hygiene even if one is not done properly. Now, it is you who has to take care of you, no more orders from mom or dad, you are well past that age.

Relationships are affected due to bad habits. Your marital life might be in trouble in case you don't practice many of the bad habits reduction. A marriage counselor might help you with these before you get married. As long as you want to keep yourself clean, no one can affect you, even in a positive way, so, think positive and stay away from thoughts that can affect your marital life.

A selfish attitude lies top on the list of bad habits. This will give a bad idea about you to others, but keep your preferences right, don't let everyone in front just to look nice, this will make them trample you. So, keep in mind that you are the only person who can possibly influence your thoughts.

Keep in mind the possible ways to avoid every other bad habit. Change, for the good, before that bad habit engulfs your character. It is hard to avoid every other bad habit, but it always feels good to keep it minimal.

Nicotine Withdrawal: Simple Solution For Smokers

Most smokers will find it difficult to quit smoking because they are addicted to nicotine which is the major component of cigarette. And when they are ready to quit they must prepared themselves for adverse effects of nicotine withdrawal which gives unpleasant symptoms.

The symptoms includes craving for tobacco, anxiety, poor concentration, irritability, restlessness, stomach upset, drowsiness, and occasional headache. Also there is possible of weight gain and depression for those that use tobacco to control weight. There are lots of ways by which you can prevent such unpleasant symptoms by finding replacement for nicotine. These can be done using medical, physical and psychological methods.

Medically, you can use drug to deal with the nicotine withdrawal symptoms and you have to start on exact date you picked to quit. If you smoke when you are depressed before, you can replace that with antidepressant when you decide to stop smoking. You can also use anxiolytics and nicotine gums.

As a matter of fact many prefer nicotine gum because nicotine allows them to titrate their own rate of nicotine absorption through the buccal mucosa. Make sure you don't chew it immediately after eating food or drinking soda because for nicotine absorption there is a need for neutral pH and you can have that when you just eat or drink.

Apart from nicotine gum you can use transdermal patch, which is more convenient for delivering nicotine. There are different dosing strategies for transdermal patch. Though, none of the strategies are superior to the other. They are either a single stable dose or a decreased dome which may be used every 2 weeks. The patch is often used for 6 weeks.

Alternatively you can use nasal spray instead of gum or patch. It's a nicotine inhaler and it looks very much like a cigarette holder. It has nicotine impregnated with menthol. It will give you immediate relief from nicotine withdrawal symptoms.

Apart from using nicotine replacement drugs, physical exercise can help you as well.

You can control weight gain and reduce crave for tobacco through daily physical exercise. Just like you need to consult your physician when thinking of nicotine replacement drugs, you need to contact your physician too to know more about the best physical exercise for you.

How Good Habits Can Turn Into Bad Habits

It is not uncommon for good habits to morph into bad habits. This often happens when good habits are taken to an extreme. This is why people should be aware of their behavior, even when it might seem positive.

People who want things to be the very best can seem to be very upbeat people. At least that is true until they go too far. When their leadership becomes nit-picking perfectionism, their good habits have turned into bad habits. Once it has reached such a point, it is hard to salvage the situation.

Sometimes people make their neatness into bad habits. They start out nice enough. They just want to keep things tidy and clean. They are perfectly willing to do some work to keep it that way. Then, they go overboard. They begin stressing over every tiny smudge or speck of dust. Besides this, they expect you to be as obsessive as they are.

There are two of these situations that are fairly similar. People turn good savings practices into bad habits. The first is when a person starts saving money for emergencies or for the future. They start a savings account, or an investment account. Then they begin to put money into it.

If they develop bad habits, they can get carried away with their savings and become a miser. They can be that person who will not buy their children new school clothes because the money has to go into savings. They can be the one who will drive a car that breaks down every week. They cannot bear spending money that could go to savings.

A similar situation happens when people start buying in bulk. At first they tell themselves they are just stocking up. However, the stocking up may not stop at a reasonable level. If it has become a bad habit, their entire basement, garage, attic, and all their closets may be filled with extra food and cleaning supplies. They have so much that it will go bad before they can possibly eat it all.

You may wonder how being concerned about others can possibly lead to bad habits. A person who is this thoughtful is generous in spirit and cares only for the well-being of those around her. The bad habit may come in when the person puts others' needs too far above her own. This can lead to all sorts of psychological problems for her.

Perhaps you have heard that there is never a dumb question. People are generally encouraged to ask questions at school and at work. However, it becomes a bad habit when people ask questions aimlessly to no purpose. They will sometimes ask so many questions that no work can be accomplished at all. Sometimes it is better to try to figure something out on your own.

This just goes to show that extremes are usually bad habits waiting to happen. Be a considerate person, yes, but do not do it at the expense of your own well-being. Indeed, you should maintain a savings account. Just make sure your family has what it needs. Do not let your good habits turn into bad habits and make your life difficult.

Bad Habits Can Be Expensive

Bad habits can be very expensive to maintain. Never mind that they are annoying to others. Do not think about the pain you cause yourself, if you do not want to. Just remember that your bad habits are hitting you where it hurts-in your wallet.

Smoking has always been a bad habit to have. In past times, people smoked more cigarettes, but cigarettes were cheaper. Now, many people have cut down on the number of cigarettes they smoke per day. Yet, those few are more expensive now than the many were back then. That's accounting for inflation, too.

This is because lawmakers have seen fit to put large taxes on cigarettes. In many areas, the taxes are set to go up even higher. Some states are planning hikes of $10 per carton. If that will not stop you from smoking, what will?

Alcohol, too, is a bad habit that is subject to sin tax. It depends on how expensive your taste in alcohol is whether it will cost you more or less. Usually, most people will go to drinking less expensive alcohol as their dependency grows. However, it is not unusual for someone to go to a bar on a Friday night and spend their paycheck on alcohol.

Many people get into bad habits of taking prescription drugs when they have an injury, such as a back injury. They may be given muscle relaxants and strong pain relievers to get them through the first painful days. This is a reasonable medical response to their condition.

Yet, the medication helps them feel so good that they will want to get more. They may go back to the doctor to get more. If the doctor will not agree, they may go to different doctors to get different prescriptions. All these doctor visits and prescriptions usually come with a price tag. Then, when that no longer works, they will go to get their pain relief medications on the streets. It will cost even more to keep up their bad habits.

Of course, people who have bad habits with illegal drugs probably have some of the most expensive bad habits of all. Whether it is cocaine, heroin, marijuana, or methamphetamine, there are no cheap drugs. At least, there will not be an unlimited supply of cheap drugs. If a person truly has a bad habit with one of these drugs, they will always want more until they quit. The cost can get to be astronomical.

Gambling can lead people into financial hardship. Some people have such bad habits with gambling that they lose their houses and everything else they own. They may be in staggering debt on top of that. Now that there is online gambling, they cannot even get away from their bad habits by staying home.

Shopaholics spend money like there is no tomorrow. This bad habit can destroy a budget. It can take money away from things that need to be paid, like a mortgage or car payment.

It is clear that these bad habits are costly in the short run. Many of them are also costly over time, as health issues settle in. The cost of cigarettes is high, for example, but the cost of lung cancer is very much higher. Ridding yourself of these bad habits can only help your finances to get better.

Medical Treatments For Bad Habits

Medical treatments can be of some help to some bad habits. There are people who have overcome many bad habits through medical treatments. There are rehabilitation centers that actually make you cut down on your bad habits like smoking and alcoholics.

Nicotine replacement therapy is basically the cure for smokers. The nicotine patches need to be used in order to reduce smoking, which is a very bad and a dangerous habit. These nicotine patches can be stuck to your skin and then it can be forgotten till the day ends. A person with morning cravings is suggested to keep the patch on through the night.

Nicotine gum is the next best thing and famous thing that is being used by people. This is more useful for people who prefer doing things with their mouth. This also cuts the need to smoke. All you need to do is place the gum between the cheeks and the gum after chewing for sometime. The nicotine enters your bloodstream. The nicotine lozenges also work the same way.

There are nasal sprays and inhalers that contain nicotine. These can be obtained in stores with the correct prescription from the doctor. The spray sends in nicotine immediately into the system. Using the inhaler is as good as smoking, but it is not too dangerous.

It is not possible to cheat when being treated with a nicotine patch. If you smoke while having your patch on, then you might end up suffering from high blood pressure, thus putting your health in danger.

The medications from the prescription are used to relieve the destruction of many bad habits. Zyban is still being used as an aid to stop smoking. This medicine is something that can keep you away from depression. It also eliminates one's urge to smoke.

Zyban can be used along with nicotine patches; it will not do much damage to your health, not even close to what was being done by smoking. Survey shows that many people have accepted that they are not really thinking of smoking while using these medications.

There is a newer version of medication for those trying to quit smoking. Chantrix. it makes smoking a less pleasurable exercise once you start consuming it. Chantrix is even more effective than Zyban. Apart from relieving you of the smoking addiction, it is said to be effective even with addiction to alcohol. This is quite an effective medication, because people smoke and drink in similar situations.

Gambling is another addiction that keeps the adults too engaged to even realize that they are being cheated upon. Gamblers may be having some physical base for this. So, a new medication is being studied to prevent people from gambling.

Methadone has been a very effective medication for over three decades now. It basically controls all the relapsing symptoms after people quit heroin and other drugs. Methadone has a very successfully compiled history.

It has been proved that addictive behavior has been stopped by constant medication. This is not something that can be done within a day; it takes some undaunted efforts to achieve success.

Research About Bad Habits

Bad habits keep following you wherever you go, in some form. There are many reasons for people to start practicing bad habits. There are several ways to quit this. Several researches in the past few years have rendered results.

When people researched what is the basic motivation for people to actually quit habits that are bad, it gave the answer that it is more because of emotional reasons that people have. The successful ones are the ones who wanted to quit it badly, and succeeded, those who don't even think of it, don't succeed.

Knowledge is best only when it is used to influence a person's emotional balance. For instance, if a person sets up a wide network to actually help people quit smoking, he uses his mind to influence his emotions. The penalties because of the bad habits influence the emotional balance of a person that makes them want to quit.

A research was conducted on the habitual behavior of the brain. Researches tested them with rats. Rats were made to run through a maze, which had a chocolate in the other end. The rat was learning the way through the maze, and responded to all information.

After sometime, the brain responded only to the starting and the ending points. This is exactly the response that our brain gives, when our brain gets used to the bad habits. It keeps focusing on its reward.

After sometime, they removed the chocolate. Then, basal ganglia started responding to all the parts in the maze. This is exactly like quitting all the bad habits to live every moment in life.

After sometime the chocolate was put back in place, the basal ganglia started responding to the starting and ending point as before. Then, the brain again got back to the addiction, as the object was put back in place. This is exactly like the bad habits resurfacing.

A study was conducted to check the extent to which people were ready to get over the old habits and replace them with new habits. This test was conducted by testing using word tests and memorization. The research checked if the people learnt new associations after grasping similar associations first.

The test was concluded, and the results were interesting. The habits that were learnt first were below the level of consciousness, and more automatic. Stress made people revert back to old habits.

There was a study related to risky behavior, and what people think about it. This survey was conducted in several parts of Canada to learn what the most dangerous thing to do was. Most of the people actually accepted that overeating, smoking and drinking were all considered most dangerous. The health habits were the most risky habits other than the thoughtless behavior.

It is really important to learn how to react and tackle bad habits. The more information one knows, greater are the chances for them to learn the ways to get over them. With all the research being put in, the bad habits might be kicked out of the system pretty soon.

Looking to get your hands on more great books?

Come visit us on the web and check out our great collection of books covering all categories and topics. We have something for everyone.

http://www.kmspublishing.com

Made in the USA
Lexington, KY
08 February 2013